To My
dear Friend & M[...]
Carmen.

Although this is not the "official"
Tao, it might be a nice start.
May it bring good thoughts & actions
which result in positive payback
100-fold to you – you most
certainly deserve it. Metta.

Namasté –
Nina.

THE TAO OF
MOM

Also by Taro Gold

What Is Love?
A Simple Buddhist Guide to Romantic Happiness

Open Your Mind, Open Your Life
A Book of Eastern Wisdom
(Large Second Volume)

Open Your Mind, Open Your Life
A Little Book of Eastern Wisdom
(Miniature First Volume)

Please visit www.TaroGold.com to learn more
about the author and his work.

THE TAO OF
MOM

*The Wisdom of Mothers
from East to West*

TARO GOLD

**Andrews McMeel
Publishing**

Kansas City

With deepest thanks to Mom
and every woman
who has stood proudly
as a lighthouse of the heart
in guiding others
toward truly joyful lives

ISBN: 0-7407-3958-1

Library of Congress Control Number: 2003112409

04 05 06 07 08 TWP 10 9 8 7 6 5 4 3 2

Book design by Holly Camerlinck
Illustrations by Matthew Taylor

INTRODUCTION

A myriad of moms influence our lives—from biological and adoptive mothers and relatives to family friends, favorite teachers, authors, entertainers, and leaders in social, spiritual, and political arenas. Whoever we are, we all have moms.

This small book, filled with big wisdom, is for you to give to the moms in your life, for moms to give to you, for everyone to give to dads (as a loving reminder of how wise moms can be), and of course for you to give to yourself. It's called *The Tao of Mom*, and it's a book for everyone because it's meant to help us all live happier lives.

Everyone is looking for happiness. Every day. Always.

However we define happiness—wealth, status, a sense of security or achievement—our search for happiness guides our actions and colors our perspectives. Entire libraries of huge books examine this quest in mind-bending detail. What we need are simple signs to point us in the right direction and show us when we're getting closer.

This unique collection is filled with just such helpful guideposts. It's a rare treasury of uplifting and thought-provoking quotations from both Eastern moms and Western moms (who also have Eastern sensibilities), from both celebrity moms and celebrated moms (they're all celebrated, yes?), and from mom figures in my extended family tree.

My life has been blessed with strong, insightful women guiding my path. Foremost is Mom, who encouraged me to chronicle the wisdom I gained from people I met and books I read. To promote this healthy habit, each New Year's Day she gifted me with a crisp new journal (thanks, Mom!). From those now dog-eared volumes, I've carefully selected 365 of my favorite quotations from 140 women around the world to create *The Tao of Mom*.

A few of the exceptional women included in this volume did not raise children of their own, yet all helped raise countless individuals through their outstanding examples. They lived their lives with the spirit of selfless giving, of bettering themselves and others, and of making our world a happier and safer place in which to live. To me, that is the true definition of motherhood—as expansive and inclusive as the word *tao* itself.

Tao (pronounced da-oh) is a Chinese word that means "path" or "way" and also implies "teachings" or "wisdom." *The Tao of Mom*, then, is *The Way of Mothers*, which to me represents the way of wisdom, the way of courage, and the way of compassion. It is a flow of knowledge, insight, and experience passed down through generations; a natural sense of wisdom we all share—a universal truth of humanity.

Whether you're a mother, a daughter, a father, or a son, may each of the following pages serve to inspire and enrich your own reserves of wisdom, courage, and compassion; your very own *Tao of Mom*.

母の道

The Tao of Mom

You will be happier when you stop thinking,
I'll be happier when . . .
—*Mom*

᪥

The intelligent believe only half of what they hear,
and the wise know which half.
—*Great-Grandma Edi*

᪥

We write our own destiny; we become what we do.
—*Madame Chiang Kai-shek*

᪥

Embrace simplicity.
—*Okaa-san*

$\mathcal{T}$he work will wait while you show the child the rainbow;
the rainbow won't wait while you do the work.
—*Patricia Clafford*

❧

$\mathcal{D}$o your best in all you do—not because
the task is worth it but because you are.
—*Mom*

❧

$\mathcal{I}$t is difficult to find happiness within
and impossible to find it without.
—*Kaneko Ikeda*

*T*he heroes of the next war will be those
who prevent it.
—*Great-Grandma Edi*

✌

*W*hat really matters is not whether we have problems
but how we go through them.
—*Rosa Parks*

✌

*D*o not choose for others
what you would not choose for yourself.
—*Alima Oyun*

✌

*K*eep good company, and wisdom grows.
With good friends, even the foolish become wise.
—*Kisagotami*

$\mathcal{E}$ducation must start from birth.

—*Maria Montessori*

ℰ

$\mathcal{E}$verything you want to become on the outside
you must first become on the inside.

—*Mom*

ℰ

$\mathcal{T}$he more we sweat for peace,
the less we bleed in war.

—*Vijaya Lakshmi Pandit*

ℰ

$\mathcal{W}$e don't see things as they are,
we see them as we are.

—*Anaïs Nin*

Since your idea of fulfillment is your own creation,
you must be the one who creates your own fulfillment.

—*Mom*

❧

How one wins reveals much of one's character.
How one loses reveals all of it.

—*Obaa-san*

❧

As your intention goes, so goes your reward.

—*Nirmala Sundari*

❧

Humanity will thrive when the world
appreciates the value of diversity.

—*Indira Gandhi*

*I*gnoring the facts never changes the facts.
—*Mom*

❧

*T*he surest way to remember an experience is to try to forget it.
—*Hikari Agata*

❧

*T*iming is everything. Even a terrible mistake
can become a blessing if the timing is right.
—*Obaa-san*

❧

*I*f you wish to find happiness, do good. If there is something
you can do for others, step forward and volunteer.
If you put off that opportunity, you are letting your own chance
for happiness slip away from you.
—*Elsie Tu*

*H*ow you spend your time reveals your priorities.
—*Aunt Kimiko*

❧

*E*ven the most capable one was once a beginner.
—*Mom*

❧

*W*ater can clearly mirror the sky so long as its surface is undisturbed. Likewise, the mind can reflect a true image of Self only when fully at peace.
—*Indra Devi*

❧

*W*ith wisdom, people can create success out of failure. Without wisdom, success can create failures out of people.
—*Miri Konewa*

*T*he strongest force in the world is gentleness.
—*Han Suyin*

*W*hat you teach your children you also teach your children's children.
—*Great-Grandma Edi*

*T*here is always more than meets the eye.
—*Lady Murasaki Shikibu*

*O*ur shortcomings irritate us most when we perceive them in others.
—*Mom*

*P*rejudice is often no more than a lazy person's substitute for thinking.
— *Aunt Tomee*

೪

*H*umanity is not divided into two opposing camps of good and evil.
It is made up of those who are capable of learning and
those who are incapable of learning. By learning, I mean the process
of absorbing lessons in life that enable us to increase
peace and happiness in our world.
— *Aung San Suu Kyi*

೪

*W*e are all a reflection of our mothers' secret poetry
as well as their hidden anger.
— *Audre Lorde*

೪

*T*o know oneself is to gain the most valuable knowledge.
— *Obaa-san*

10

*W*hen we are under the power of evil,
it is not felt as evil but as a necessity, or even a duty.
—*Simone Weil*

❧

*Y*ou cannot shake hands with a clenched fist.
—*Indira Gandhi*

❧

O friend, understand
The heart
Is like the sea,
Hiding treasures
All its own.
—*Mirabai*

❧

*C*onscience is what makes a boy tell his mother before his sister does.
—*Great-Aunt Iko*

*O*nly in growth, reform, and change, paradoxically enough,
is true security to be found.
—*Anne Morrow Lindbergh*

❧

*I*f you're not happy without it, you won't be happy with it.
—*Mom*

❧

*T*he spirit of youth is constant and alive. It never deserts one,
even in the face of the greatest suffering.
—*Diki Tsering*

❧

*T*he end does not justify the means. No one's rights can be secured
by the violation of other people's rights.
—*Ayn Rand*

"Do or die." This mantra is imprinted on my heart.
—Kastur Gandhi

&

It is good to have an end to journey towards,
but it is the journey that matters in the end.
—Ursula K. Le Guin

You must dream your wildest dreams to realize
what is beyond your wildest dreams.
—*Okaa-san*

*W*hen a pair of magpies takes flight together,
they envy not a pair of phoenixes.
—*Lady Ho*

*T*he greatest form of control is self-control.
—*Mom*

*I*f you seek harmony, disregard the faults of others and examine
your own faults. See no one as a stranger. Learn to make the
entire world your own. Indeed, this whole world is your own.
—*Sarada Devi*

Only through justice for all will the world know security for all.
—*Aditi Maya Rai*

C_2

Do not follow where the path may lead.
Go instead where there is no path and leave a trail.
—*Muriel Strode*

C_2

Modesty is the art of encouraging others
to find out for themselves how wonderful you are.
—*Fumiko Hayashi*

C_2

With every deed you are sowing a seed,
though the harvest you may not see.
—*Ella Wheeler Wilcox*

*D*ifficulties, opposition, criticism—these things are meant to be overcome, and there is a special joy in facing them and coming out on top. It is only when there is nothing but praise that life loses its charm.

—*Vijaya Lakshmi Pandit*

*P*erhaps there is nothing in the world so painful
as feeling that one is not valued.

—*Sei Shonagon*

*C*hildren become the kinds of people their best teachers
convinced them they could become.

—*Mom*

*I*f given a choice, I would have certainly chosen to be who I am:
one of the oppressed instead of one of the oppressors.

—*Miriam Makeba*

$\mathcal{M}$y mother taught me that people should be judged by the respect they have for themselves and others. Her words helped me do the hard things I had to do later in life.

—*Rosa Parks*

❧

$\mathcal{Y}$our past is your history, not your identity.

—*Okaa-san*

❧

$\mathcal{N}$othing in life is to be feared. It is only to be understood.

—*Marie Curie*

❧

$\mathcal{D}$on't be surprised if, when people collaborate with others, they tend to regard their own contributions as the most important.

—*Yang Chiang*

A mother's influence lasts forever.
—*Japanese proverb*

❧

*D*reams grow peace.
—*Aunt Kimiko*

❧

*T*o be actively disciplined, a child must first learn the difference between *good* and *evil*; and the task of the educator lies in seeing that the child does not confound *good* with *immobility*, and *evil* with *activity*.
—*Maria Montessori*

❧

*F*ear should never prevent you from doing what you know is right.
To be inhibited from doing what you know is right,
that is truly dangerous.
—*Aung San Suu Kyi*

*A*buse is cyclical. To break the cycle, it is up to those
who have been abused to never abuse others,
the oppressed to never oppress others.
—*Mangala Sharma*

❧

*P*ut your ear down close to your soul and listen hard.
—*Anne Sexton*

❧

*I*f you don't love what you're doing, start doing what you love.
—*Mom*

❧

*P*eople who don't get into scrapes are a great deal
less interesting than those who do.
—*Lady Murasaki Shikibu*

$\mathcal{T}$here is no substitute for hard work.

—*Okaa-san*

$\mathscr{C}$

$\mathcal{W}$hy is it that as the world becomes more "civilized,"
we need more locks, keys, and passwords?

—*Great-Grandma Edi*

$\mathscr{C}$

$\mathcal{T}$he process of maturing is an art to be learned,
an effort to be sustained. By the age of fifty you have made yourself
what you are, and if it is good, it is better than your youth.

—*Marya Mannes*

$\mathscr{C}$

$\mathcal{L}$oneliness is a choice.

—*Toora Miah*

*M*orality is the most essential characteristic of humanity.
—*Yeshe Tsogyel*

❧

*E*very political good carried to the extreme must be productive of evil.
—*Mary Wollstonecraft*

❧

*A*lways hold your head high.
—*Aunt Tomee*

❧

*W*here I was born and where and how I have lived is unimportant.
It is what I have done with where I have been that should be of interest.
—*Georgia O'Keeffe*

❧

*T*ruth isn't always beauty, but the hunger for it is.
—*Nadine Gordimer*

21

$\mathcal{M}$om prominently displayed these guideposts on the mantel of our home while I was growing up:

If a child lives with shame, he learns to feel guilty.

If a child lives with respect, he learns to feel dignity.

If a child lives with criticism, he learns condemnation.

If a child lives with praise, he learns acceptance.

If a child lives with discrimination, he learns prejudice.

If a child lives with fairness, he learns justice.

If a child lives with deceit, he learns to be dishonest.

If a child lives with integrity, he learns to be honorable.

If a child lives with ignorance, he learns to be fearful.

If a child lives with knowledge, he learns to be hopeful.

If a child lives with animosity and hate, he learns to find evil in the world.

If a child lives with friendship and love, he learns to find good in the world.

*T*he best time to give advice to children is when they are still young enough to believe that you know what you're talking about.

—*Great-Aunt Iko*

§

*I*f one lets fear, hate, or anger take possession of the mind, they become self-forged chains.

—*Helen Gahagan Douglas*

§

*B*ecome the hero of your own story.

—*Obaa-san*

§

*W*hatever is bringing you down, get rid of it. Because you'll find that when you're free, your true creativity, your true self comes out.

—*Tina Turner*

23

*M*any people have a wrong idea of what constitutes real happiness.
It is not attained through self-gratification but through
fidelity to a worthy purpose.
—*Helen Keller*

&

*N*ever put anything in your body that does not help your body.
—*Mom*

&

*M*y grandfather once told me there are two kinds of people:
those who do the work and those who take the credit. He told me
to try to be in the first group; there is much less competition.
—*Indira Gandhi*

&

*T*oo many women in too many countries speak
the same language of silence.
—*Anasuya Sengupta*

When you refrain from saying what must be said simply because it might hurt others' feelings, this is false compassion. It may appear compassionate on the surface but in the end helps no one. Furthermore, it is often only to save ourselves discomfort that we do not say or do what we must.

—Aunt Kimiko

❧

Those who have done little are sure little can be done.

—Great-Grandma Edi

❧

Our greatest accomplishments are always the victories we win over ourselves.

—Mom

❧

You must do the thing you think you cannot do.

—Eleanor Roosevelt

*G*et rid of the tendency
to judge yourself
above
below
or equal to others.
— *Abhirupa-Nanda*

❧

*C*ontentment is necessary; self-satisfaction is detrimental.
To be content includes knowing we are in the right place at the
right time to facilitate our growth. To be self-satisfied means that
we no longer realize the need for growth.
— *Ayya Khema*

❧

*N*ever compare yourself with others. If you must compare yourself
with someone, compare yourself today with yourself yesterday.
— *Aunt Kimiko*

Always try to do more than you think you can.
—*Obaa-san*

Once you have been into space, you appreciate how small and fragile the Earth is. This small, blue, shining planet, more beautiful than any other. We must not allow it to be covered by the black ash of war. All people everywhere must join hands and make peace happen. We are all riding on Spaceship Earth together.
—*Valentina Tereshkova*

*T*he love of power is strong. The power of love is stronger.
—*Mom*

❧

*T*here is no such thing as creative hate.
—*Willa Cather*

❧

*N*o one can claim to be a religious person who gives money
for the building of warships and arsenals.
—*Belva Lockwood*

❧

*I*n a way winter is the real spring, the time when the inner things happen.
—*Edna O'Brien*

❧

*W*e can only perceive in others the qualities we already possess.
—*Mom*

*W*hen you point a finger at someone else,
remember that three of your fingers point back at you.
—*Motherly proverb*

⚜

*I*f education remains along the same antiquated lines
of a mere transmission of knowledge, there is little to be hoped from
it in bettering humanity's future.
—*Maria Montessori*

⚜

*L*et go of judgment.
—*Obaa-san*

⚜

*G*overn the clock, be not governed by it.
—*Golda Meir*

*T*he future is the past come home to roost.
—*Bawei Yang Chao*

*R*umors aren't convincing
until they have been officially denied.
—*Aditi Maya Rai*

*E*verything nourishes what is already strong.
—*Jane Austen*

*O*uter beauty is temporary. Inner beauty is eternal.
—*Great-Grandma Edi*

*C*reativity is the real fountain of youth.
—*Aunt Tomee*

We are frightened by our own solitude. Yet only in solitude can we learn to know ourselves, learn to handle our own eternity of aloneness. And love from one being to another is when two solitudes come nearer, to recognize and protect and comfort each other.

—*Han Suyin*

⚮

Dare to do the things and reach for the goals in your life that have meaning for you as an individual, doing as much as you can for everybody, but not worrying if you don't please everyone.

—*Lillian Gordy Carter*

⚮

Loving someone is not the same as knowing someone.

—*Toora Miah*

⚮

It is time we realized that the future of this planet and the beings it houses depends on the promotion of the welfare of all.

—*Ramakrishnan Rajalakshmi*

The soul, like the moon, becomes new,
and always new again.
—*Lalleswari*

Jealousy is not born of love! It is a child
of selfishness and distrust.
—*Hamishuma*

Nothing in this world is permanent. Though a
rainbow may appear stationary against the sky, it
vanishes in an instant. Though the flowers of
spring bloom with brilliant luster, that beautiful
sight will vanish with the change of season.
Though a girl like me has health and energy
beyond measure, like all others I cannot control
the time of my departure.
—*Princess Mandarava*

When the going gets rough, those who dwell on the past will give up. Those who focus on the future can always find the hope and strength to persevere.

—*Mom*

❧

The vices of the rich and great are mistaken for errors; and those of the poor and lowly, for crimes.

—*Lady Marguerite Blessington*

❧

Shame kills faster than disease.

—*Buchi Emecheta*

❧

Whatever becomes familiar becomes acceptable.

—*Aunt Kimiko*

*H*ave you ever noticed that life consists mostly of interruptions,
with occasional spells of rushed work in between?
—*Buwei Yang Chao*

❧

*T*hose who do not avert their eyes from the question of death realize
just how precious and irreplaceable life is. They cannot fail to devote
every minute of their lives to developing and improving themselves.
—*Jutta Unkart-Seifert*

❧

*C*haracter cannot be developed in ease and quiet.
Only through experience of trial and suffering can the soul
be strengthened, ambition inspired, and success achieved.
—*Helen Keller*

❧

*W*here there is unseen virtue there will be visible reward.
—*Great-Aunt Iko*

*T*he clearer your goals the better—like aiming at a target. The more focused you are on the target, the more likely your chance of striking it.
—*Jeanny Chen*

Education should not merely be a means for earning a living or an instrument for acquiring wealth. It should be an initiation into the life of spirit, a training of the human soul in the pursuit of truth, and the practice of virtue.
—*Vijaya Lakshmi Pandit*

*T*he words that parents write on the hearts of their children nothing can ever erase.
—*Great-Grandma Edi*

*T*reat your loved ones as you do your pictures,
and place them in their best light.
—*Jennie Jerome Churchill*

&

A loving partnership is more a shared direction
than a shared emotion.
—*Mom*

&

*N*ever doubt that a small group of thoughtful,
committed citizens can change the world; indeed,
it's the only thing that ever has.
—*Margaret Mead*

&

*H*onest dreams are always possible.
—*Obaa-san*

36

The hardest thing for a person to bear is not an insult or a beating, but loneliness, ostracism.

—Ru Zhijuan

❧

Foolish are those who treat their loved ones blandly, even rudely, then go out and smile false pleasantries at every stranger they meet.

—Great-Grandma Edi

❧

People's reputations depend mostly on what others don't know about them.

—Lady Ho

❧

The immediate is often the enemy of the ultimate.

—Indira Gandhi

*T*rue and lasting peace on this planet will come through waves of human revolution. Unlike any in history, this revolution will be based on a profound transformation of people's hearts; a fundamental awakening in which we change from lives spent hurting ourselves and others to lives spent helping ourselves and others.

—*Mom*

❧

*T*here is no chance, no destiny, no fate that can hinder or control the firm resolve of a determined soul.

—*Ella Wheeler Wilcox*

❧

*P*erception is everything. If we have a cup full of water and I ask, "Is this cup full?" you will say, "Yes, it is full." If I pour the water out and ask again, "Is this cup full?" you will say, "No, it is empty." But the cup is still full; it is now full of air.

—*Obaa-san*

In the last analysis, all revolutions must be social revolutions,
based upon fundamental changes in society;
otherwise it is not revolution, but merely a change of government.
—*Madame Sun Yat-sen*

❧

Don't be surprised when a child's adolescence
begins before a father's adolescence ends.
—*Great-Aunt Iku*

❧

Somewhere along the line of development we discover who we
truly are, and then we make our real decision for which we
are responsible. Make that decision primarily for yourself because
you can never live anyone else's life, not even your child's.
The influence you exert is through your own life
and who you become yourself.
—*Eleanor Roosevelt*

No one has yet realized the wealth of sympathy, the kindness and generosity hidden in the soul of a child. The effort of every true education should be to unlock that treasure.

—Emma Goldman

Your body controls your health.
Your mind controls your body.
You control your mind.

—Mom

Whatever you would have your children become, strive to exhibit in your own lives and conversation.

—Lydia H. Sigourney

Mothers understand what children do not say.

—Jewish proverb

*W*omen's liberation is the liberation of the feminine in the man
and the masculine in the woman.
—*Corita Kent*

🎕

*N*o matter what accomplishments you make, somebody helps you.
—*Althea Gibson*

🎕

*A*s long as the civilized world allows inhuman treatment
to be inflicted upon any people, then our freedom
is threatened as well.
—*Rosa Parks*

🎕

*B*e like the sun—supportive, warm, and life-affirming—
wherever you go.
—*Aunt Tomee*

$\mathcal{K}$ind words can be short and easy to speak,
but their echoes are endless.

—*Mother Teresa*

❧

$\mathcal{S}$olitude is the salt of personhood.
It brings out the authentic flavor of every experience.

—*May Sarton*

❧

$\mathcal{F}$ollow these simple guidelines for a happy life:
First, figure out who you are; second, be you;
third, figure out what you want to do; fourth, do it.

—*Mom*

❧

$\mathcal{O}$ur mothers always remain the strangest,
craziest people we've ever met.

—*Marguerite Duras*

I'd rather see you poor men's wives, if you were happy, beloved, and contented, than queens on thrones, without self-respect and peace.

—*Louisa May Alcott*

❧

*A*bout the time a woman thinks her work as a mother is done, she becomes a grandmother.

—*Great-Grandma Edi*

❧

*W*e must have perseverance and above all confidence in ourselves. We must believe that we are gifted for something and that this thing must be attained.

—*Marie Curie*

❧

*T*he compassion of those who love humanity is stronger and deeper than the ocean.

—*Jutta Unkart-Seifert*

*A*t a crucial moment, follow your heart instead of your mind. Your mind relies on calculation and subjective information. It will sometimes favor actions that hurt you. Your heart relies on instinct and wisdom. It will always favor actions that benefit you. If you can't tell the difference between your inner voices of heart and mind, look back at any actions you regret. Those came from your mind.

—*Obaa-san*

&

*T*he surest way to relieve your sadness
is to ease the sadness of others.
—*Aunt Kimiko*

&

*W*e teachers can only help the children's work going on,
as servants wait upon the master.
—*Maria Montessori*

The tigress is wise; she uses her full strength no matter the strength of her opponent.
— *Anandabai Joshee*

❧

No man chooses evil because it is evil;
he only mistakes it for happiness, the good he seeks.
— *Mary Wollstonecraft*

❧

You must honestly love yourself
before you can honestly love another.
— *Ho Shuang-ch'ing*

❧

I suppose leadership at one time meant muscles;
but today it means getting along with people.
— *Indira Gandhi*

*W*hen others are mistaken, express areas of agreement
before explaining why they are wrong.
—Great-Aunt Iko

CO

*S*ometimes we look so intently toward the pinnacle
that we stumble over the steps leading to it.
Development begins just where you are.
—Mrs. Herman Stanley

CO

*C*hildren especially need love when they appear to least deserve it.
—Mom

CO

*B*oth art and life are derived from the power that reigns in the
universe. This power is truth—the truth that has always been. Artists
don't create art or beauty, we just discover what was already there.
—Younhee Paik

46

*M*ay the extraordinary days of your past
be the common days of your future.
—*Great-Grandma Edi*

❧

*T*he young do not know enough to be prudent,
and therefore they attempt the impossible—and achieve it,
generation after generation.
—*Pearl S. Buck*

❧

A teacher is ten times more respectable than a helper,
a father a hundred times more than a teacher, and a mother
a thousand times more than a father.
—*Brahman proverb*

❧

*W*e study in youth, we understand with age.
—*Ohaa-san*

47

No emotion is as busy yet unproductive as jealousy.

— *Alima Oyun*

✿

Arrogance stifles one's development.

— *Aunt Kimiko*

*G*ossip is beneath you.
—*Mom*

&

A common cure for all of our hindrances is noble friends
and noble conversations, which are health food for the mind.
—*Ayya Khema*

&

*A*lways hang on to hope. It is one of life's most precious treasures—
an endless wellspring of joy.
—*Great-Grandma Edi*

&

*C*reative minds have always been known to overcome
any kind of bad training.
—*Anna Freud*

Peace in the world requires that we recognize the real enemies of humanity and work to vanquish them. These enemies are war, ignorance, disease, poverty, hunger, environmental pollution, and the wasting and ruination of the world's resources by militarism. These are the imperatives on which we must focus our energies and abilities if we wish to secure humanity's survival.

—*Ava Helen Pauling*

A bright future is a present earned in the past.

—*Aunt Tomee*

Life begets life. Energy begets energy.
It is by spending oneself that one becomes rich.

—*Sarah Bernhardt*

Do not do what you would undo if caught.

—*Hannah Arendt*

*I*dentifying one's weak points is a springboard
for developing one's strength.
—*Kaneko Ikeda*

❧

*A*ll love that has not friendship for its base
is like a mansion built upon the sand.
—*Ella Wheeler Wilcox*

❧

*T*o take good care of others you must first take good care of yourself.
—*Mom*

❧

A person can be imprisoned, but an idea cannot.
A person can be exiled, but an idea cannot.
A person can be killed, but an idea cannot.
—*Benazir Bhutto*

The best and most beautiful things in the world cannot be seen
or even touched—they must be felt with the heart.

—*Helen Keller*

To the hopeless, life is like a closed book.
To the hopeful, life is like a book waiting to be opened.

—*Ohaa-san*

Never help a child with a task at which she feels she can succeed.

—*Maria Montessori*

There are no hopeless situations; there are only people
who have grown hopeless about them.

—*Clare Boothe Luce*

If at first you don't succeed,
try doing it the way your mother told you.
—*Great-Grandma Edi*

✌

In times of crisis we must show men our courage.
If we are brave, they will be brave.
—*Kastur Gandhi*

✌

Real education should educate us out of self into something finer;
into a selflessness that links us with all humanity.
—*Lady Nancy Astor*

✌

While we all hope for peace it shouldn't be peace at any cost,
but peace based on principle, on justice.
—*Corazon Aquino*

*D*iplomacy is the art of erasing others' mistakes
instead of highlighting them.
—*Great-Grandma Edi*

☙

*P*overty? Wealth? Seek neither—one causes swollen bellies,
the other, swollen heads.
—*Kassiane*

☙

*S*ince there's positive in even the worst of us,
and negative in even the best of us, it's hardly fit for any of us
to talk about the rest of us.
—*Great-Aunt Iko*

☙

*T*hose who are content with themselves require little from others.
—*Obaa-san*

*W*e must make our homes centers of compassion
and forgive endlessly.
—*Mother Teresa*

*I*f you have a great ambition, take as big a step as possible in the
direction of fulfilling it. The step may only be a tiny one, but trust
that it may be the largest one possible for now.
Mildred H. McAfee

*O*ne must go against the stream when the stream is unjust.
—*Mom*

I am convinced that we must train not only the mind,
but the heart and hand as well.
—*Madame Chiang Kai-shek*

$\mathcal{O}$nly as high as I reach can I grow,
Only as far as I seek can I go,
Only as deep as I look can I see,
Only as much as I dream can I be.

—Karen Ravn

※

$\mathcal{A}$s the mother is, so is her child.

—Asian proverb

※

$\mathcal{T}$he fragrance always stays in the hand that gives the rose.

—Hada Bejar

*D*o good, and never mind to whom.
—*Great-Grandma Edi*

❧

*H*ow quickly the locks rust, the hinges grow stiff,
on the doors we close behind us!
—*Lady Murasaki Shikibu*

❧

*F*reedom is not for the timid.
—*Vijaya Lakshmi Pandit*

❧

*I*t's far better to marry the one you are happy with
than the one you are not happy without.
—*Aunt Tomee*

*H*ow you love shows who you are.
—*Mom*

ℰℓ

*T*he past must inspire the future. Our young people must understand and appreciate their history, for in doing so they construct an unshakable identity that allows them to live good lives and to advance the cause of human rights that is so dear to us all.
—*Rosa Parks*

ℰℓ

*I*t is never too late to be who you might have been.
—*George Eliot*

A life is for one generation. A reputation is forever.
—*Honnamma*

❧

*N*ever give up trying to do what you really want to do.
Where there are dreams, love, and inspiration, you can't go wrong.
—*Ella Fitzgerald*

❧

*F*or a long time it seemed to me that real life was about to begin,
but there was always some obstacle in the way. Something had to be
got through first, some unfinished business; time still to be served,
a debt to be paid. Then life would begin. At last it dawned on me
that these obstacles were life.
—*Bette Howland*

❧

*P*eople can understand the causes and effects of the human
comedies and tragedies of their times by studying history.
—*Zhang Kangkang*

$\mathcal{A}$n absence of rainy days in life makes for a desert in the heart.
—*Mom*

&

$\mathcal{F}$ew people are willing to make wholehearted commitments,
which is why few accomplish great transformations in their lives.
—*Obaa-san*

&

$\mathcal{L}$ove the moment, and the energy of that moment
will spread beyond all boundaries.
—*Corita Kent*

&

$\mathcal{I}$t is your joyful right and honorable duty to exceed
your parents' abilities in every way possible.
—*Kaneko Ikeda*

*L*uck is not chance, it's toil.
Fortune's expensive smile is earned.
—*Emily Dickinson*

❧

*R*elationships are 10 percent how you make them,
90 percent how you take them.
—*Mom*

❧

*N*o love is as faithful or beneficial as self-love.
—*Ohaa-san*

❧

*H*uman rights means the chance for everybody
to make the most of themselves.
—*Lillian Gordy Carter*

When trouble occurs, avoid wasting time and energy determining who did this or that or how or why—the most important thing is what you are going to do about it.
—Great-Grandma Edi

❦

Some people make anger, rather than a deeply held belief, the basis of their actions. They don't mind damaging society as a whole in the pursuit of their immediate objective. No society can survive if it yields to the demands of anger, whether of the few or the many.
—Indira Gandhi

❦

It is organized violence at the top that incites individual violence at the bottom.
—Emma Goldman

*T*hose who prepare for war get it.
—*Winifred Holtby*

℘

*T*he same energy of character that renders a man a daring villain
would have rendered him useful to society,
had that society been well organized.
—*Mary Wollstonecraft*

℘

*L*iberty and equality are the two inalienable rights of the individual.
—*Madame Sun Yat-sen*

℘

*T*he present is that short interval when the future pauses
for a moment before becoming the past.
—*Miri Konewa*

No one can build his security upon the nobleness of another person.
—Willa Cather

GX

Courage is the price that life exacts for granting peace.
The soul that knows it not, knows no release
From little things;
Knows not the livid loneliness of fear
Nor mountain heights, where bitter joy can hear
The sound of wings.
—Amelia Earhart

GX

There is no shortcut to self-improvement.
—Alima Oyun

GX

Character isn't inherited. One builds it daily by the way
one thinks and acts, thought by thought, action by action.
—Helen Gahagan Douglas

*D*on't be surprised when, by the time you learn the answers,
your questions have changed.

—*Great-Aunt Iko*

❧

*L*ove with insight is far better than love at first sight.

—*Mom*

❧

*M*ore important than knowing what you are capable of doing
is knowing what you are not capable of doing.

—*Lucille Ball*

65

*Y*ou always have time for the things you put first.
—*Obaa-san*

⪊

*I*f your heart did not break now and then, how would you know it is there? Hearts break, then mend, and break and mend again in a cycle without beginning, without end. As surely as the dawn sows the evening, as surely as the twilight sows the morn.
—*Bette Bao Lord*

⪊

*E*very beetle is a gazelle in the eyes of its mother.
—*Moorish proverb*

⪊

*C*haracter is who you are; reputation is who others think you are.
—*Great-Grandma Edi*

*T*o know how to say what other people only think,
is what makes poets and sages; and to dare to say what others
only dare to think, makes martyrs or reformers.
—*Elizabeth Rundle Charles*

❧

*C*reativity can be described as letting go of certainties.
—*Gail Sheehy*

❧

*T*he hypocrite's crime is that he bears false witness against himself.
What makes hypocrisy the vice of vices is that integrity can indeed
exist under the cover of all other vices except this one.
—*Hannah Arendt*

❧

*T*he world needs artists who creatively compose with compassion
more than missionaries who destructively crusade against reality,
who want to turn the clock back to an ideal past that never was.
—*Han Suyin*

We plant seeds that will flower as results in our lives,
so best to remove the weeds of anger, avarice, envy, and doubt,
so that peace and abundance may manifest for all.

—*Dorothy Day*

❧

If three out of four things you try fail, try four times more things.

—*Okaa-san*

❧

The intelligent always know what to say;
the wise always know what not to say.

—*Mom*

❧

Just as a mother at the risk of her own life
loves and protects her child, her only child,
so let you cultivate boundless compassion
for all that exists throughout the universe.

—*Buddhist proverb*

I consider the world my motherland, and every war to me
has the terror of a family feud.

—*Helen Keller*

❧

*R*espect breeds friendship.
Friendship breeds trust.
Trust breeds peace.

—*Mom*

*M*any things we need can wait. The child cannot.
Now is the time his bones are being formed;
his blood is being made; his mind is being developed.
To him we cannot say tomorrow. His name is today.
—*Gabriela Mistral*

*C*ultivate within you that rarest form of intelligence: common sense.
—*Aunt Tomee*

*P*eace is inextricably linked with our love and respect
for Mother Earth.
—*Coretta Scott King*

*L*earning is not attained by chance. It must be sought for
with ardor and attended to with diligence.
—*Abigail Adams*

*A*void letting success go to your head.
Avoid letting failure go to your heart.
—*Great-Grandma Edi*

❧

*T*he cure for boredom is curiosity. There is no cure for curiosity.
—*Dorothy Parker*

❧

*I*t's such a grand thing to become the mother of a mother
that the world calls her a grandmother.
—*Obaa-san*

❧

*E*stablishing lasting peace is the work of education;
the most politics can do is keep us out of war.
—*Maria Montessori*

*H*appiness is not a goal, it's a by-product.
—*Eleanor Roosevelt*

If it's painful for you to criticize your friends,
you're safe in doing it; if you take the slightest pleasure in it,
that's the time to hold your tongue.
—*Alice Duer Miller*

A fortress of powerfully positive thoughts on the inside
will protect you even on the outside.
—*Mom*

It is easy to be popular. It is not easy to be just.
—*Rose Elizabeth Bird*

Don't fall in love with others for who they could become.
Fall in love with others for who they are.
—*Aunt Kimiko*

꧁

Joy can spring like a flower even from the cliffs of despair.
—*Anne Morrow Lindbergh*

꧁

Blessed are those who can give without remembering,
and take without forgetting.
—*Elizabeth Bibesco*

꧁

If you don't want your children to hear what you're saying,
pretend you're talking to them.
—*Great-Aunt Iko*

*O*ne of the hardest things to do
in this world is to reveal a hidden love.
—*Ho Shuang-ch'ing*

❧

*L*ove and marriage should be like creating
successive works of art.
—*Fumiko Hayashi*

❧

*J*oy is the best cosmetic.
—*Great-Grandma Edi*

❧

*L*ife may not always be fair, and not always
just, but even so it is always important to
continue working for what you believe in.
—*Benazir Bhutto*

$\mathcal{W}$e seek in our surroundings a reflection of our inner selves.
—*Mom*

❧

$\mathcal{A}$ nation's peace and stability depend upon the
relationships created in each household.
—*Jade Snow Wong*

❧

$\mathcal{L}$ittle evil would be done in the world
if evil could never be done in the name of good.
—*Marie von Ebner-Eschenbach*

❧

$\mathcal{F}$ailure is not falling down;
it is staying down once you have fallen.
—*Obaa-san*

A leader who doesn't hesitate before sending a nation into battle is not fit to be a leader.
—*Golda Meir*

*I*t is justice, not charity, which is lacking in the world.
—*Mary Wollstonecraft*

*R*esiding within you are treasures of instinctual wisdom inherited from your mother and father, and from countless mothers and fathers before them.
—*Great-Grandma Edi*

*E*ducation is not some rarified art. It is simply engaging children with gentleness and kindness, and motivating them so that they will have an interest in learning for themselves.
—*Elsie Tu*

*W*e all had a mother who underwent the pain of childbirth to bring us into the world. Life passes from mother to child, from mother to child. Behind each of us is the love of an infinite number of mothers—mothers who wish for nothing more than that we, their children, live good lives. The Earth is filled with the sound of these mothers' prayers.

—*Valentina Tereshkova*

❧

*W*henever I held my newborn babe in my arms, I used to think what I did and what I said to him would have an influence, not only on him, but on everyone he meets, not for a day or a year, but for all eternity. What a challenge, what a joy!

—*Rose Fitzgerald Kennedy*

❧

*M*others should befriend their children's friends.

—*Sara Delano Roosevelt*

*C*ompassion is what makes people truly human.
—*Mom*

❧

*T*he ability to deceive oneself is the most insidious of talents.
—*Great-Grandma Edi*

❧

*P*eople spend years creating multibillion-dollar business proposals, thesis papers, and so on. They solicit input, collect data, induce, deduce, compare, research, and discover. . . . Your life is much more valuable and important than all such matters, so why don't you do the same for your life? You should by all means scrupulously design and create a fundamental life proposal that will benefit you for all eternity.
—*Jeanny Chen*

❧

*F*oolish are they indeed who trust luck!
—*Lady Murasaki Shikibu*

Because our cultures are different doesn't mean we can't get along.
In fact, it's often the differences that allow us to learn
from one another and help one another.
—*Le Hoa Lam*

❧

You will learn that in dealing with things, you spend more time
and energy dealing with people than in dealing with things.
—*Buwei Yang Chao*

❧

Reject social currents that value the valueless.
—*Aunt Tomee*

❧

No matter how big a nation is,
it is no stronger than its weakest people.
—*Marian Anderson*

You may travel the world over in search of what you desire,
only to find it upon returning home.
—*Ohaa-san*

❧

The power to question is the basis of all human progress.
—*Indira Gandhi*

❧

Right decisions come from experience,
and experience comes from wrong decisions.
—*Great-Aunt Iko*

❧

Let no one ever come to you without leaving better and happier.
—*Mother Teresa*

*C*herish your traditions. They are the creators of your spirit
and your pride, and the backbone of your sensibilities.
They make you who you are and define what you want to be.
—*Diki Tsering*

♋

*W*e are rich only through what we give.
—*Anne-Sophie Swetchine*

♋

*S*ocial progress is merely a gradual falling in line
with the ideas of the minority.
—*Aditi Maya Rai*

♋

*I*t is not enough to simply "live and let live." Genuine tolerance
requires an active effort to understand other people's points of view.
—*Aung San Suu Kyi*

When you have a sore spot on your body, you may avoid feeling it, for you despise the pain. Yet discomfort is a valuable sign that something has gone wrong. You should seek to understand the source of your discomfort, for therein lies the path to comfort. This holds true for both body and soul.

—Mom

❧

There is no king who has not had a slave among his ancestors, and no slave who has not had a king among his.

—Helen Keller

❧

If we could raise one generation with unconditional love, there would be no war.

—Elisabeth Kübler-Ross

❧

One moment of hate can erase a lifetime of happiness.

—Aunt Tomee

*T*he worst barbarity of war is that it forces men collectively to commit acts against which individually they would revolt with their whole being.

—*Ellen Key*

৶

*W*hen will our consciences grow so tender that we will act to prevent human misery rather than avenge it?

—*Eleanor Roosevelt*

৶

*T*ruth and nonviolence must be our watchwords.

—*Kastur Gandhi*

৶

*E*liminate within whatever would create violence without.

—*Great-Grandma Edi*

The mind is the seat of all good and evil.
—Yeshe Tsogyel

❧

Anger is often but an echo of anguish.
—Mom

❧

The cure for anything is salt water—sweat, tears, or the sea.
—Karen Blixen

❧

Mountains are steadfast but mountain streams
Go by, go by
And yesterdays are like rushing streams,
They fly, they fly
And great heroes famous for a day,
They die, they die.

—Hwang Chin-I

84

When we experience loss, we naturally feel sad. All things, however, must come and go. Everything and everyone in this world are either emerging into appearance or moving toward disappearance. When we realize this, we can better appreciate the good in our lives here and now.

—Obaa-san

&

People who do not know how to weep with their whole heart do not know how to laugh either.

—Golda Meir

&

The externals are simply so many props; everything we need is within us.

—Etty Hillesum

&

What is there to fear? Life? Death? Just roll with the punches.

—Wakako Yamauchi

*H*ad there been no difficulties and thorns in the way,
humanity would have remained in its primitive state
and made no progress in civilization or culture.
— *Anandabai Joshee*

&

A greater loss than one's death is the death
of one's curiosity while living.
— *Obaa-san*

&

*T*o find a rare jewel is easy. To find a good spouse is difficult.
— *Yü Hsüan-chi*

&

*H*ow a comfortable life can improve one's tolerance of others!
— *Wang Anyi*

$\mathcal{N}$othing is ever entirely as one would expect. I'm a vegetarian.
The Dalai Lama eats meat. Go figure.
—Great-Aunt Iko

$\mathscr{C}$

$\mathcal{Y}$ou are truly an adult when you start worrying
about younger generations.
—Aunt Kimiko

$\mathscr{C}$

$\mathcal{A}$s the traveler who has once been from home is wiser
than he who has never left his own doorstep, so knowledge of one
other culture should sharpen our ability to scrutinize more steadily,
to appreciate more lovingly, our own.
—Margaret Mead

$\mathscr{C}$

$\mathcal{T}$he bridges of intercultural friendship have a unique construction;
the more people cross over them, the stronger they become.
—Mom

*Peace we want, because there are other wars
to fight against poverty, disease, and ignorance.*
—Indira Gandhi

❧

The way of progress is neither swift nor easy.
—Marie Curie

❧

Good luck often follows those who don't include it in their plans.
—Great-Grandma Edi

❧

When you forget the beginner's awe, you start to decay.
—Lady Nobuko Albery

❧

A mother's goodness is deeper than the sea.
—Japanese proverb

*G*ossiping about people is a waste of time.
Speak instead of ideas.
—*Ohaa-san*

💫

*I*t's not how old you are, but how you are old.
—*Marie Dressler*

💫

*E*ach friend represents a world in us, a world possibly not born until
they arrive, and it is only by this meeting that a new world is born.
—*Anaïs Nin*

💫

*P*eople have been grouped, classified, and labeled.
But how can labels express the complications of humanity?
After all, superficial differences are not so important.
—*Huang Zongying*

89

*I*t is always easier to make people cry or gasp
than to make them think.
—*Golda Meir*

❧

*Y*esterday is experience; tomorrow is hope; today is bridging the two.
—*Aunt Tomee*

❧

*Y*ou are not responsible for everything;
you are only responsible for yourself.
—*Great-Grandma Edi*

❧

I have noticed that when the children of wealthy families, assured
of any titles and emoluments they desire, receive praise no matter how
little they have done to deserve it, they fail to see any advantage in
fatiguing themselves by arduous and exacting studies.
—*Lady Murasaki Shikibu*

*W*ealth covers sin—the poor are naked as a pin.
—*Kassiane*

🕮

*T*here is no absolute freedom in the world. Freedom is always relative.
—*Zhang Jie*

🕮

*O*ne rarely sees the major toil that precedes even minor achievements.
—*Aunt Kimiko*

🕮

A minute of thought is worth more than an hour of talk.
—*Mom*

🕮

I do not want the peace that brings understanding;
I want the understanding that brings peace.
—*Helen Keller*

*A*dolescence is a time of life when we are well informed about anything we are not required to study.
—*Great-Aunt Iko*

✌

*I*t's strange, but now that I have my own money, I don't feel like spending it.
—*Hikari Agata*

✌

*Y*our greatest teacher is your own heart.
—*Mom*

✌

*D*ifficulties are not necessarily unfortunate. It depends on your attitude. You can either let difficulties crush you, or you can use them to build your strength.
—*Indira Gandhi*

*H*uman beings are more important than scientific truths.
— *Ava Helen Pauling*

⁊

*W*e ourselves feel that what we are doing is just a drop in the ocean.
But the ocean would be less without that drop.
— *Mother Teresa*

⁊

*B*iology is the least of what makes someone a mother.
— *Oprah Winfrey*

⁊

*P*erhaps travel cannot prevent bigotry, but by demonstrating
that all peoples cry, laugh, eat, worry, and die, it can introduce
the idea that if we try to understand each other,
we may even become friends.
— *Maya Angelou*

The wise always expect the unexpected.
—*Obaa-san*

☙

To have ideas is to gather flowers;
to think is to weave them into garlands.
—*Anne-Sophie Swetchine*

☙

The daily exercise of common sense is a form of genius.
—*Mom*

☙

If the populace marches in file, that's your signal to
break from the ranks. If a thousand generations did thus and so,
that's your cue to do otherwise.
—*Muriel Strode*

*H*ate must be learned.
Love needs no instruction.
—*Great-Grandma Edi*

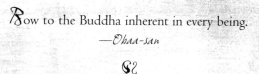

*T*o think deeply and to be fully alive are the same.
—*Hannah Arendt*

*B*ow to the Buddha inherent in every being.
—*Obaa-san*

*I*f there is a faith that can move mountains, it is faith in your own power.
—*Marie von Ebner-Eschenbach*

*T*he most important things in life are not things.
—*Mom*

$\mathcal{T}$he truest greatness lies in being kind,
the truest wisdom in a happy mind.
—*Ella Wheeler Wilcox*

$\mathcal{C}2$

$\mathcal{A}$ppreciate each moment,
for each moment creates your life.
—*Aunt Tomee*

$\mathcal{C}2$

$\mathcal{L}$et's create a world in which children will
someday ask us, "What was war?"
—*Great-Grandma Edi*

*Your state of being is far more important
than your state of doing.*
—*Mom*

❧

*And the day came when the risk to remain tight in the bud
was more painful than the risk it took to blossom.*
—*Anaïs Nin*

❧

Mom recited the following passage, one of her favorites from the
Lotus Sutra, each day while I was growing up:
Let this be my constant thought—
How I can help all living beings
to follow their highest potential
and quickly attain enlightenment,
Nam-myoho-renge-kyo.
Nam-myoho-renge-kyo.
Nam-myoho-renge-kyo.

BIOGRAPHICAL NOTES

Abhirupa-Nanda (circa 550 B.C.E.) Indian poet and one of Shakyamuni Buddha's first women disciples.

Abigail Adams (1744-1818) Considered the first women's rights leader of the United States, she was the wife of President John Adams, and mother of President John Quincy Adams.

Hikari Agata (1943–1992) Japanese author.

Lady Nobuko Albery (b. 1941) Japanese author and historian.

Louisa May Alcott (1832–1888) U.S. author best known for her classic novel *Little Women*.

Marian Anderson (1897–1993) First African American to be named a permanent member of the Metropolitan Opera Company. She was appointed an alternate UN delegate in 1958.

Maya Angelou (b. 1928) U.S. author, poet, educator, actress, and civil rights advocate. Best known for her series of autobiographical novels beginning with *I Know Why the Caged Bird Sings*.

Corazon Aquino (b. 1933) First woman president of the Philippines who, while serving from 1986 to 1992, restored democracy to her country after twenty years of dictatorship.

Hannah Arendt (1906–1975) Jewish German author, political scientist, and teacher. She was forced to flee with her family to France during World War II, eventually settling in the United States.

Lady Nancy Astor (1879–1964) First woman member of the British Parliament. Born in the United States, she married Waldorf Astor and later assumed his seat in the House of Commons.

Aung San Suu Kyi (b. 1945) Preeminent leader in Myanmar of the movement to reestablish democracy in that country. While under house arrest in 1991 she won the Nobel Peace Prize.

Jane Austen (1775–1817) British author who wrote her first novel at age fourteen and created classics such as *Pride and Prejudice* and *Sense and Sensibility* before dying of Addison's disease at age forty-one.

Lucille Ball (1911–1989) U.S. media producer and actress. Considered the world's best-known woman comedian, she pioneered television's situation comedy format and won four Emmys.

Sarah Bernhardt (1844–1923) French actress and playwright.

Benazir Bhutto (b. 1953) First woman in modern history to lead a Muslim nation, serving as Pakistan's prime minister from 1988 to 1990 and from 1993 to 1996.

Elizabeth Bibesco (1897–1945) British author.

Rose Elizabeth Bird (1936–1999) U.S. judge who became the first woman chief justice of California.

Lady Marguerite Blessington (1789–1849) British author and socialite.

Karen Blixen (Isak Dinesen) (1885–1962) Danish author who in 1914 moved to East Africa, where she remained until 1931. From her experiences she wrote the autobiographical novel *Out of Africa*.

Pearl S. Buck (1892–1973) Author and women's rights advocate. Raised in China by U.S. parents, she learned Chinese before English and was educated by a Confucian scholar. Her novel *The Good Earth* won a Pulitzer Prize in 1932, and she won the Nobel Prize in literature in 1938.

Lillian Gordy Carter (1898–1983) U.S. nurse, civil rights adovate, and mother of President Jimmy Carter. She worked for many years to eliminate segregation in her native Georgia. At age sixty-eight she served in India as a member of the Peace Corps.

Willa Cather (1873–1947) U.S. author, editor, and teacher. She won the Pulitzer Prize in 1923 for *One of Ours*.

Buwei Yang Chao (1889–1981) Chinese author and physician.

Elizabeth Rundle Charles (1828–1896) British author, painter, musician, and poet.

Jeanny Chen (b. 1951) Essayist and Nichiren Buddhist practitioner. A Taiwanese émigré to the United States, she is the inspiration and organizing force behind the international Buddhist resource Web site www.HappyJeanny.com.

Madame Chiang Kai-shek (1897–2003) Chinese sociologist, reformer, educator, and former first lady of Taiwan (Republic of China).

Jennie Jerome Churchill (1854–1921) U.S.-born British author and mother of Winston Churchill.

Marie Curie (1867–1934) Polish-born French scientist who became one of the greatest scientists of the twentieth century, winning two Nobel Prizes—in physics in 1903 and in chemistry in 1911. She performed pioneering studies with radium and contributed profoundly to the understanding of radioactivity.

Dorothy Day (1897–1980) U.S. journalist and student of Gandhism, known as "the grand old lady of pacifism." Cofounder of *The Catholic Worker* and creator of the House of Hospitality network of homeless shelters.

Indra Devi (1899–2002) Yoga's most prominent female force for more than sixty years. After living in India for many years, she moved to Shanghai to open her first school of yoga in 1940. She spent the rest of her life teaching yoga around the world.

Sarada Devi (1853–1920) Brahman spiritual leader regarded by some as a saint.

Emily Dickinson (1830–1886) Considered one of the greatest U.S. poets of all time.

Helen Gahagan Douglas (1900–1980) U.S. actress who entered politics in 1944, becoming a three-term congresswoman, and later worked with the United Nations in foreign relations.

Marie Dressler (1869–1934) Canadian American actress.

Marguerite Duras (1914–1996) Born and raised in Vietnam by French parents. Her best-known novel and autobiographical story, *The Lover*, won France's most prestigious literary award, the Goncourt Prize, in 1984.

Amelia Earhart (1897–1937) U.S. aviation pioneer, and the first woman to cross the Atlantic by plane. In 1937 she attempted to fly around the world, but she was lost on the flight between New Guinea and Howland Island.

Marie von Ebner-Eschenbach (1830–1916) Austrian author.

Great-Grandma Edi (1892–1996) Women's rights advocate, independent businesswoman, and Taro Gold's great-grandmother.

George Eliot (Mary Ann Evans) (1819–1880) Considered the preeminent female British author of all time.

Buchi Emecheta (b. 1944) Nigerian author whose works are often viewed as sociological statements that examine the universal female condition, although they speak specifically for Nigerian women struggling against traditional mores that limit progress.

Ella Fitzgerald (1917–1996) U.S. jazz singer known as the "first lady of song." She is considered the world's best-known jazz and popular artist. She recorded 150 albums and won thirteen Grammys.

Anna Freud (1895–1982) Austrian pioneer in child psychoanalysis and daughter of Sigmund Freud.

Indira Gandhi (1917–1984) Only child of India's first prime minister, Jawaharlal Nehru. In 1966 she became the first woman prime minister of India and remained in office until 1977. She served again from 1980 until she was assassinated in 1984.

Kastur Gandhi (1869–1944) Indian social reformer and wife of Mohandas K. "Mahatma" Gandhi.

Althea Gibson (1927–2003) U.S. tennis champion. In 1957 she became the first black player to win at Wimbledon and was named the Associated Press Female Athlete of the year.

Emma Goldman (1869–1940) Russian-born Jewish American lecturer, political organizer, feminist, and editor. Founder of *Mother Earth* magazine.

Nadine Gordimer (b. 1923) South African author who won the Nobel Prize in literature in 1991.

Han Suyin (b. 1917) Chinese physician and author.

Fumiko Hayashi (1904–1951) Japanese author.

Etty Hillesum (1914–1943) Dutch Jewish author who died in Auschwitz at the age of twenty-nine.

Lady Ho (circa 300 B.C.E.) Chinese poet and noblewoman.

Ho Shuang-ch'ing (1712–?) Chinese poet.

Winifred Holtby (1898–1935) British author and pacifist who lectured widely advocating creation of the League of Nations, precursor to the United Nations.

Honnamma (1662?–1699) Indian poet and servant to King Chikkadevaraja. Educated by a royal scholar, she was named "Goddess of Charming Literature." Her works are still sung in India today.

Bette Howland (b. 1937) U.S. author.

Huang Zongying (b. 1925) Chinese actress, researcher, and author.

Humishuma (1888–1936) Okanogan author. Her book, *Cogewea: The Half-Blood*, published in 1927, is one of the first novels written by a Native American woman.

Hwang Chin-I (1506–1544) Korean poet.

Kaneko Ikeda (b. 1932) Japanese women's leader, peace activist, homemaker, and wife of the Buddhist philosopher and author Daisaku Ikeda, founder of Soka University and the worldwide Buddhist association Soka Gakkai International.

Great-Aunt Iko (1916–1992) Homemaker, beauty salon owner, Soka Gakkai Buddhist teacher, and Taro Gold's great-aunt.

Anandabai Joshee (1865–1887) First Hindu woman and first Indian woman to earn a medical degree.

Kassiane (circa 825) Byzantine poet.

Helen Keller (1880–1968) U.S. author and lecturer. Blind and deaf from infancy, she studied under Anne Sullivan, later becoming an inspiration to countless people around the world.

Rose Fitzgerald Kennedy (1890–1995) U.S. author and mother of President John F. Kennedy and Senators Robert and Edward Kennedy.

Corita Kent (1918–1986) U.S. muralist and printmaker.

Ellen Key (1849–1926) Swedish author.

Ayya Khema (1923–1997) Buddhist author and teacher, born to Jewish German parents who escaped to China during World War II. Later imprisoned in a Japanese war camp, she survived to study Buddhism in Asia and teach Eastern spirituality around the world.

Aunt Kimiko (b. 1934) Homemaker, Soka Gakkai Buddhist teacher, and Taro Gold's aunt.

Coretta Scott King (b. 1927) U.S. human rights advocate and, along with her late husband, Dr. Martin Luther King Jr., a student of Gandhism. She has worked around the world on behalf of racial justice, women's equality, gay rights, nuclear disarmament, and ecological responsibility.

Kisagotami (circa 550 B.C.E.) Cousin of Shakyamuni Buddha and one of his first women disciples.

Miri Konewa (1917–1991) Maori homemaker.

Elisabeth Kübler-Ross (b. 1926) Swiss-born U.S. psychiatrist and pioneer in the study of death and dying. Known for her framework describing the experience of dying, which progresses through denial, anger, bargaining, depression, and acceptance.

Lalleswari (1360–1399) Kashmiri poet considered by some to be a saint. She pioneered interfaith dialogue and greatly influenced the thought and lives of her contemporaries. Her words are frequently used in Kashmiri maxims, and her messages continue to resonate in Kashmir today.

Le Hoa Lam (b. 1960) Vietnamese-born Australian politician.

Ursula K. Le Guin (b. 1929) U.S. science fiction author. Born to distinguished anthropologist parents, she grew up surrounded by Eastern philosophy texts and ethnographic studies. Her novels are known for their detail and internal logic.

Anne Morrow Lindbergh (1906–2001) Author and aviation pioneer. First licensed U.S. woman glider pilot and Charles Lindbergh Jr.'s copilot, navigator, radio operator, and wife. In 1931 they journeyed in a single-engine plane over uncharted routes from Alaska to Japan and China.

Belva Lockwood (1830–1917) First woman admitted to the Bar of the U.S. Supreme Court. While studying law she worked as a teacher to support her family as a single mother. A strong civil rights advocate, she represented mostly women, Native Americans, and the poor.

Bette Bao Lord (b. 1938) Chinese-born U.S. author.

Audre Lorde (1934–1992) Author, poet, educator, and gay rights advocate born to West Indian parents in New York. She was known for dedicating her life to social justice on every front.

Clare Boothe Luce (1903–1987) U.S. author, feminist, playwright, and diplomat. She served as a congresswoman in the 1940s and ambassador to Italy in the 1950s.

Miriam Makeba (b. 1932) South African singer known as Mama Africa around the world.

Princess Mandarava (circa 700 B.C.E.) Daughter of the king of Zahor, ruler of north India. When her father demanded she give up Buddhism to marry, she left the palace to live as a commoner. In time the king accepted his daughter's philosophy and built a special palace for the study of Buddhism.

Marya Mannes (1904–1990) U.S. author and journalist.

Mildred H. McAfee (1900–1994) U.S. educator and military officer. She became president of Wellesley College in 1936 and in 1942 the first woman line officer in the U.S. Navy.

Margaret Mead (1901–1978) U.S. anthropologist, author, and museum curator. Proponent of the theory that personality is formed through cultural conditioning.

Golda Meir (1898–1978) Considered by many to be the mother of the modern state of Israel. As the first woman prime minister of Israel, she was hailed internationally for her initial diplomatic efforts to bring peaceful resolutions to Middle East conflicts.

Toora Miah (1931–1988) Aboriginal Australian homemaker.

Alice Duer Miller (1874–1942) U.S. author, poet, and teacher.

Mirabai (1450–1547) Indian poet, noblewoman, and wife of the heir apparent to the ruler of Mewar. She left the court in her thirties to become a wandering mendicant. Her words remain popular throughout India today.

Gabriela Mistral (1889–1957) Chilean educator, cultural minister, diplomat, and poet. In 1945 she became the first Latin American woman to win the Nobel Prize in literature.

Mom (b. 1941) Independent businesswoman, kitchen table philosopher, Soka Gakkai Buddhist teacher, and Taro Gold's mother.

Maria Montessori (1870–1952) First Italian woman to receive a medical degree. She moved to India during World War II; there she studied Eastern philosophy, opened schools, and trained hundreds of teachers in her method. She is considered to have revolutionized the world of education.

Lady Murasaki Shikibu (978?–1026?) Japanese author and poet who many scholars believe authored the world's first novel, *The Tale of Genji*, circa 1007. She was a member of the powerful Fujiwara clan and a lady-in-waiting to Empress Akiko.

Anaïs Nin (1903–1977) French-born U.S. author, lecturer, and diarist.

Obaa-san (1916–1997) Japanese Tea Master, Wabi Sabi philosopher, Soka Gakkai Buddhist teacher, and Taro Gold's grandmother.

Edna O'Brien (b. 1932) Irish author and short story writer.

Georgia O'Keeffe (1887–1986) Considered one of the most compelling U.S. painters of the twentieth century. Her representations of beautiful North American landscapes served as a counterpoint to the often chaotic images embraced by the art world at the time.

Alima Oyun (b. 1951) Mongolian social leader and teacher.

Younhee Paik (b. 1955) Korean artist and painter.

Vijaya Lakshmi Pandit (1900–1990) Indian diplomat and international peace advocate. Along with her brother, Jawaharlal Nehru, the first prime minister of India, she was a friend of Mahatma Gandhi. She was elected president of the UN General Assembly in 1953, the first woman to hold the position.

Dorothy Parker (1893–1967) U.S. poet, humorist, and writer.

Rosa Parks (b. 1913) Considered the mother of the modern U.S. civil rights movement. In 1955 she refused to give up her seat on a Montgomery, Alabama, bus. That simple act of courage set in motion a chain of events that would forever change race relations in the United States.

Ava Helen Pauling (1903–1981) U.S. homemaker, human rights advocate, and wife of Linus Pauling. She worked for Japanese American rights during World War II, and in 1962 her husband shared with her his Nobel Peace Prize for her efforts to promote world peace and ban nuclear weapons.

Aditi Maya Rai (b. 1961) Nepalese homemaker and teacher.

Ramakrishnan Rajalakshmi (b. 1926) Indian biochemist, nutritionist, and educator. She is known for her work in nutrition with UNICEF.

Ayn Rand (1905–1982) Russian Jewish author, philosopher, and founder of Objectivism. After witnessing the Russian Revolution begin in 1917, she dreamed of leaving for the United States. In 1926 she obtained a visa to visit relatives in Chicago and never returned to Russia.

Eleanor Roosevelt (1884–1962) U.S. civil rights advocate and wife of President Franklin D. Roosevelt. She was elected head of the UN Human Rights Commission in 1946, immediately drafting the Universal Declaration of Human Rights, and became a member of the NAACP board of directors in 1956.

Sara Delano Roosevelt (1854–1941) Mother of President Franklin Roosevelt. The daughter of a wealthy tea trader in China, she grew up in both Hong Kong and New York. She remained a strong influence on her son, supervising his education and later serving as his close adviser.

Ru Zhijuan (b. 1925) Chinese author and mother of the author Wang Anyi.

May Sarton (1912–1995) Belgian-born U.S. author, poet, teacher, and gay rights advocate.

Sei Shonagon (967–1013?) Japanese author, descendant of Emperor Temmu, and lady-in-waiting to Empress Sadako. Her *Pillow Book* is considered one of the finest works of Japanese literature.

Anasuya Sengupta (b. 1974) Indian social activist and poet.

Mangala Sharma (b. 1969) Bhutanese refugee leader.

Gail Sheehy (b. 1937) U.S. journalist, author, editor, and cultural observer.

Lydia H. Sigourney (1791–1865) U.S. teacher, author, poet, and philanthropist. She used proceeds from her writings for charitable causes including peace societies and missions for the poor.

Muriel Strode (1875–1945?) U.S. author.

Madame Sun Yat-sen (1893–1981) Chinese civil rights advocate, lecturer, and political leader.

Nirmala Sundari (circa 550 B.C.E.) One of Shakyamuni Buddha's first women disciples.

Anne-Sophie Swetchine (1782–1857) Russian French author.

Mother Teresa (1910–1997) Born in Macedonia as Agnes Gonxha Bojaxhiu. While attending Catholic school she realized her mission to help the poor, and at age eighteen she joined a community of nuns in Calcutta, India. She won the Nobel Peace Prize in 1979.

Valentina Tereshkova (b. 1937) Russian cosmonaut. In 1963 she became the first woman to travel in space. Her daughter, Elena, was the first child born to parents who had both traveled in space.

Aunt Tomee (b. 1932) Homemaker, Soka Gakkai Buddhist teacher, and Taro Gold's aunt.

Diki Tsering (1901–1981) Mother of Tenzin Gyatso, the fourteenth Dalai Lama of Tibet.

Elsie Tu (b. 1913) Community activist and politician. Born in Britain, she moved to China in 1947. After settling in Hong Kong in the early 1950s, she gained great popularity as a member of Hong Kong's Legislative Assembly.

Tina Turner (b. 1939) U.S. singer, actress, and Nichiren Buddhist practitioner. She is a Rock and Roll Hall of Fame inductee, and her life story inspired the Oscar-nominated movie *What's Love Got to Do with It.*

Jutta Unkart-Seifert (b. 1945) Austrian soprano, Dr.h.c. of Soka University of Tokyo, and president of the European Cultural Initiative for the Young Generation.

Wang Anyi (b. 1954) Chinese author and daughter of the author Ru Zhijuan.

Simone Weil (1909–1943) French social activist, educator, and philosopher. Born to Jewish parents, she studied the Bhagavad Gita and other Eastern philosophical texts before joining the Free French forces under Charles de Gaulle to fight Germany in World War II.

Ella Wheeler Wilcox (1850–1919) U.S. poet and journalist who said that "the art of being kind" was her religion and that she practiced it every day.

Oprah Winfrey (b. 1954) U.S. talk show host, actress, publisher, and social commentator.

Mary Wollstonecraft (1759–1797) British feminist, one of the earliest and most influential European women's rights advocates. She is the mother of Mary Shelley, author of *Frankenstein.*

Jade Snow Wong (b. 1922) Chinese American author and ceramics artist.

Wakako Yamauchi (b. 1924) Japanese American author.

Yang Chiang (b. 1911) Chinese writer, scholar, and translator.

Yeshe Tsogyel (757–817) Tibetan Buddhist princess.

Yü Hsüan-chi (843–868) Chinese poet, courtesan, and Taoist priestess.

Zhang Jie (b. 1937) Chinese author.

Zhang Kangkang (b. 1950) Chinese author.